# Dog Lovers' Poems

*with love*
*Rosemary*

23.4.06

# Dog Lovers' Poems

A collection of prose
and verse
compiled by

## Jeff Kennett

Published by
Crown Content Pty Ltd
A.C.N. 096 393 636
A.B.N. 37 096 393 636
Level 1, 141 Capel St
Nth Melbourne Vic 3051
Telephone: (03) 9329 9800
Fax: (03) 9329 9698
Internet: www.crowncontent.com.au
Email: mail@crowncontent.com.au

Copyright © 2000 Jeff Kennett

All rights reserved. This publication is copyright and may not be resold or reproduced in any manner (except excerpts thereof for bona fide study purposes in accordance with the Copyright Act) without the prior consent of the Publisher.

Every effort has been made to ensure that this book is free from error or omissions. However, the Publisher, the Authors, the Editor, or their respective employees or agents, shall not accept responsibility for injury, loss or damage occasioned to any person acting or refraining from action as a result of material in this book whether or not such injury, loss or damage is in any way due to any negligent act or omission, breach of duty or default on the part of the Publisher, the Authors, the Editor, or their respective employees or agents.

The National Library of Australia
Cataloguing-in-Publication entry:

Dog lovers' poems : a collection of prose and verse.

   ISBN 1 86350 336 6

   1. Dogs - Poetry. I. Kennett, Jeff.

821.0080362977

Cover & Page Design: Ben Graham
Artist: Mark Hilton

Printed in Australia by Brown Prior Anderson

*In memory of*

Yonkers
Banana
Elle
Tigger

*and for*

Ruby & Heide

# Contents

| | |
|---|---|
| Introduction | vii |
| In The Beginning | 1 |
| The Birth Of A Dog | 2 |
| A Doggie's Prayer | 3 |
| The Dog's Ten Commandments | 4 |
| A Dog's Prayer For His Master | 6 |
| The Prayer Of The Dog | 7 |
| The Pup Who Found God | 8 |
| What Is A Dog? | 9 |
| The New Dog | 10 |
| The Sleeping Puppy | 12 |
| I Pity The Man | 13 |
| The Christmas Gift | 14 |
| A Boy And A Dog | 16 |
| A Puppy Speaks | 17 |
| I Brought A Puppy Home One Day | 18 |
| Dog's Day | 20 |
| Dachshund | 20 |
| Four Feet | 21 |
| Dedication For A Kennel | 22 |
| Dog Day | 23 |
| Anniversary Thanks | 24 |
| The Seeing Eye | 25 |
| Whose Dog? | 26 |
| The Dog Owners If | 28 |
| With Love, Together | 30 |
| My Dog | 31 |
| Twelve Years 'On The Chain' | 32 |

| | |
|---|---|
| With Love From A Lonely Dog | 34 |
| Corgi | 35 |
| My Phantom Hand | 36 |
| Chihuahua | 37 |
| I Had A Little Dog Called Spot | 37 |
| Dogs | 38 |
| Our Dog's Gone Bananas | 40 |
| My Doggie | 42 |
| Dachshund | 43 |
| Growing Up Lament | 44 |
| The Noble Dog | 46 |
| The Complaint Of A Trained Dog | 48 |
| Spotty's Christmas | 50 |
| Pekinese | 53 |
| My Dog - Before And After | 54 |
| The Empty Kennel | 55 |
| The Dog (As Seen By The Cat) | 56 |
| The Power Of The Dog | 58 |
| Goodbye | 60 |
| An Honoured Place | 63 |
| Is There A Dog Heaven? | 64 |
| Short And Sweet | 65 |
| A Little Stray | 66 |
| Scruffy - In Memory Of | 67 |
| If It Should Be… | 68 |
| The White Dog | 70 |
| Nearly Home | 72 |
| Bella | 74 |
| Boxer | 75 |
| Brandy | 76 |
| A Poem For Dog Lovers | 77 |

| | |
|---|---|
| The Earl Of Ascot | 78 |
| Sally Dog | 80 |
| Lady | 81 |
| Fleur | 82 |
| His Apologies | 84 |
| A Piddling Pup | 86 |
| A Wag Of A Tale | 88 |
| Last Will And Testament Of A Dog | 90 |
| A Dog's Plea | 92 |
| Choc the Water Spaniel | 94 |
| I Died Today | 96 |
| Message From a Little Ghost | 98 |
| Rainbow Bridge | 99 |
| My Visit To The Surgery | 100 |
| Ode to Angus | 102 |
| Pal Of Mine | 104 |
| The Devotion of Greyfriars Bobby | 105 |
| My Friend | 108 |
| The Power of the Dog | 110 |
| The Presbytery Dog | 112 |
| To Jack The Toothless Terroriser! | 114 |
| The Rubaiyat of a Scotch Terrier | 116 |

# Introduction

In 1989, when doing a seven-week stint on Melbourne radio station 3AW as the morning host presenter, I read a number of my favourite dog poems on air.

The result was electric – a great deal of talkback about dogs, requests for more poems, requests for poems to be re-read. Many listeners sent in their favourite poems to me.

In response to many requests, I indicated that one day I would publish a collection of the poems I had received.

The first edition sold out. Now as a broadcaster on 3AK I have been asked whether we will reprint. So here it is with even more poems.

Where the authors are known, they are acknowledged.

Where they are not known, I hope they get pleasure, knowing the happiness these poems will bring to thousands of people.

For now read on and enjoy. Every dog lover and owner will quickly relate to almost every poem.

Jeff Kennett

*Jeff Kennett who was Premier of Victoria from 1992-1999, has many commercial interests, as well as chairing beyondblue, the National Depression Initiative. He is also a broadcaster on Talk 1116 3AK hosting the drive program from 4 to 6pm weekdays.*

# In The Beginning

When the first Great Cause of all things
Left Man to evolve with time
He built in a lesser body
A fragment of Love Divine.

To give to the poorest beggar
A love that makes him a King
And kiss the hand which is empty when
Friends and fortune take wing.

As a name for this rare being reflecting
The name of God,
Man spelt his creator backwards
And called his small likeness — Dog.

# The Birth Of A Dog

When the Maker was resting from labour
As he gazed on the world from above
He saw many poor, lonely humans
With no one to care for or love.

And the Lord in his infinite mercy
With compassion both tender and wise
Made a furry four-legged creature
With a tail and a pair of brown eyes.

And with a heart filled with loyal devotion
From the moment his short life began
And the Maker smiled down from his heaven
On the dog he created for man.

# A Doggie's Prayer

Please keep my master free from harm
Wherever he may be
And when this war is over
Bring him safely back to me
So we can stroll together
Or share a cosy fire.
Please hear a doggie's earnest prayer
And grant his heart's desire.

# The Dog's Ten Commandments

1. Love thy neighbour as thyself; only a bit more if he's a decent fellow.

2. Always come when you're called, but take your time over it. Use your discretion as to how long you should wait, but at the first sign that he really does mean it, return to heel immediately. It pleases him to think that he has trained you nicely.

3. Bones should always be buried. They taste much better after a day or two in the ground. Moreover, the aroma is improved with keeping.

4. Never steal food from the larder or the table unless you are quite certain that you will not be found out. Then please yourself! Re taking things off the table; I find after breakfast the ideal time. All the family have gone out of the room, attending to their various affairs, and a golden opportunity arises. I adore kippers but, if you will take my advice, avoid knocking a knife or fork off the table. I was badly caught by being clumsy enough to do this the other day - they heard it!

5. Never take the cat's food if she has a family of kittens. Cats' claws are uncommonly sharp!

6. Treat all strangers with the utmost suspicion until you have been properly introduced by Master or Missus. Even then, don't get too friendly, one never knows!

7. As long as you are properly fed, eschew the dust bin. An occasional visit, however, is good for the soul though sometimes bad for the stomach. Use discretion here; you may get into serious trouble if discovered. Castor oil is beastly stuff anyway!

8. Sleep with one eye open or you may be caught napping!

9. if you have a favourite chair, get on it as often as you can. You will be turned off many times but, occasionally, you will get your own way.

10. Remember, the Master is the boss and from him all good things come!

# A Dog's Prayer For His Master

O Lord of Humans, make my master faithful to his fellowmen
As I am to him;
Grant that he may be devoted to his friends and family
As I am to him;
May he be open- faced and undeceptive
As I am;
May he be as true to trust reposed in him
As I am to his.

Give him a face cheerful like unto my wagging tail;
Give him a spirit of gratitude like unto my licking tongue.
Fill him with patience like unto mine
That awaits his footsteps uncomplainingly for hours;
Fill him with my watchfulness, my courage, and my readiness
To sacrifice comfort or life.

Keep him always young at heart
And crowded with the spirit of play even as I.
Make him as good a man as I am a dog;
Make him worthy of me, his dog

*By Capt Will Judy*

# The Prayer Of The Dog

Lord,
I keep watch!
If I am not here
Who will guard their house?
Watch over their sheep?
Be faithful?
No one but You and I
Understands
What faithfulness is.
They call me, "Good dog! Nice dog!"
Words…
I take their pats
And the old bones they throw me
And I seem pleased.
They really believe they make me happy.
I take kicks too
When they come my way.
None of that matters.
I keep watch!
Lord,
Do not let me die
Until, for them,
All danger is driven away.
Amen.

# The Pup Who Found God

I reckoned at a glance, he'd never have a chance
Compared with pups of "proper" pedigree
Not that he hadn't any "blue-bloods", he had too many
For what is termed a kennel ancestry.

He had those doleful, wise, brown Cocker Spaniel eyes;
A Foxie tail had somehow claimed his rear,
His back with dot formation, declared him part Dalmatian,
While Pomeranian pricked up with each ear…

He sensed my pensive mind, and nosed my shoe and whined,
He hoped he'd found the "God" he'd sought at last;
I thought of price of meat, our narrow, terraced street…
My mood of "Take him home with you" had passed.

With ear, nose and tongue, the pleading little mong
Yet tried to reach my heart, I turned away;
His tail dropped in defeat, he slunk across the street,
Still looking back, a forlorn sad-eyed stray…

"Dash what they'll say", I thought, "true pals like him aren't bought from kennels. Here boy – come back", I cried.
With joyous bark he turned… the brake-locked tyres burned
I'm glad … the pup … found "God" before he died.

# What Is A Dog?

A dog is a pup you couldn't resist,
You bought the wag of his tail and the gleam in his eye,
And a few sundries you hadn't bargained for —
His fleas, his worms and his untrained bladder.
You bought a welcome home and devotion.
You bought chewed-up slippers and a dug-up garden.
You bought responsibilities and rights and trust.
You bought companionship and banished loneliness.
You bought a duty, to be as good as your dog thinks you are,
Through sickness and health, for better or for worse.
Until death do you part.

*Mary Bishop*

# The New Dog

*(My favourite poem)*

There's a new dog lying on the parlour rug
Where the old dog used to lie,
A dog with a short, white, curly coat
And a brown patch over his eye;
He takes his meals from the old dog's dish
And he sleeps in the old dog's chair,
And the rest have forgotten the Spaniel dog
Who for 10 long years slept there.

But at night when "the house is fast asleep"
Sounds a step I used to know,
And the dog that I love comes stealing back
From the land where the good dogs go;
A dark shape opens the bedroom door,
I hear a familiar whine,
There are two brown paws on the counterplane
And a dog's head close to mine.

There isn't a secret he "keeps from me"
Of life in the Great Beyond;
There are shining seraphs to take him walks,
Real bones and a splendid pond;
And the baby angels throw balls for him
In the fields where the grass grows sweet,
And he hasn't forgotten the strange brown stone
That he used to lay at my feet.

He remembers the days "in the grassy parks"
And the cats he used to chase
(And yet they talk of another dog
Who shall take the old dog's place).
He tells me he looked for the old green chair
Where his basket used to be,
But he found an intruder sleeping there
So he came to look for me.

Oh, the new dog is a faithful chap,
And he earns his daily bread,
And the right to feed from the self-same dish
And sleep on the self-same bed.
And of course he must be on the parlour rug
Where the old chap used to lie,
But a brown dog visits me every night
Pathetically asking why.

*L B Malleson*

# The Sleeping Puppy

The pup lies curled as if in sleep, his head
Rests on his paw, unyielding road his bed.
His smooth ear gently folds and from his lips
A scarlet trickle comes and slowly drips.
Gone now the running, barking, pouncing fun,
The snuggling warmth, and all the years to come,
His new-found gods betrayed his simple trust,
And cruel engine left a whirl of dust.

Where's that puppy gone? Well, I don't know,
I put him out the back an hour ago.
But did you block the hole or close his pen?
I think I did. Well, now he's out again,
Better go and look. The voices call,
The puppy cannot hear, no sound can fall
On his still mind or on his empty heart,
And all that's left awaits the council cart.

*D.S*

# I Pity The Man

I pity the man who has never known
The pleasure of owning a pup;
Who has never watched his funny ways
In the business of growing up.
I pity the man who enters his gate
Alone and unnoticed at night,
No dog to welcome him joyously home
With his frantic yelps of delight.

I pity the man who never receives
In hours of bitterest woe,
Sympathy shown by a faithful dog
In a way only he seems to know.
I pity the man with a hatred of dogs;
He is missing from life something fine;
For the friendship between a man and his dog
Is a feeling almost divine.

*May Fair*

# The Christmas Gift

The gentle arms that held me close
The quiet voice that taught me well,
But as I grew I felt them less
Instead,
There came a loneliness
Of empty days and painful nights.
Crouched in the yard, I watched
The lights that danced and twinkled so,
And people coming to and fro – with mistletoe –
But not for me …

And then one day, the house was still –
I lay amongst the heat and dust and flies
No one to heed my mournful cries
They left me on my own …
To sit and wait … and wait and sit
Until the time they saw fit
To come back home from sun and surf
With suntans and their tales of mirth,
But not for me …

I could not eat, I could not sleep,
And then I found my liberty –
I broke my chain.

It set me free.
I wandered through the heat-stained streets
My bleeding feet, my aching heart
will never understand why they
Abandoned me in such a way!
The other world seemed all ablaze
With revelry and song and love
And gifts and food and joy and fun
But not for me…

Instead, I felt the angered fists of rage
I heard the cruel unfeeling shouts
I am not wanted anywhere…
My liberty is sheer despair…

And now I lay me down to die
I know deep down no one will cry
They say a Saviour's born this day –
Perhaps it's He takes me away?

And while my soul lies bleeding here
To death upon those dancing feet
Remember all the ones like me
I was a Christmas Gift … you see?

# A Boy And A Dog

I want my boy to have a dog
Or maybe, two or three,
He'll learn from them much easier
Than he would learn from me.

A dog will show him how to love
And bear no grudge or hate,
I'm not so good at that myself
But dogs will do it straight.

I want my boy to have a dog
To be his pal and friend,
So he may learn that friendship
Is faithful to the end.

There never yet has been a dog
Who learned to double cross
Nor catered to you when you won
Or dropped you when you lost.

# A Puppy Speaks

I tripped you on the slippery floors,
And then you locked me out of doors.
You said cross words, I wonder why,
You know I love you till I die.

I know I'm just a crazy pup
Who chewed your nearest slippers up;
Though you don't like my kind of fun
I love you more than anyone.

I jumped into your favourite chair
And left my paw prints everywhere
You stomped your foot, you made me cry
And still I love you till I die.

I lie beside your bed in fright
And growl and wake you up at night
Yet this small pup would gladly give
His worthless life that you might live.

You may be right you may be wrong
But I'll be with you my whole life long
Cause I'm your pup and you're my friend
And we are buddies till the end.

# I Brought A Puppy Home One Day

I brought a puppy home one day,
It seems like only yesterday.
But it was 14 years today,
Since he first came with me to stay.
A tiny ball of energy,
I thought it would be too much for me.
My good slippers went everywhere,
Odd socks were what I had to wear.
He tore through the house and down the hall,
Nothing low was safe at all.
Suddenly, he'd fall asleep,
He looked so little, I'd start to weep.
As the weeks and months went past,
He seemed to grow so very fast.
A special bind of friendship grew,
Nothing could separate us two.
By the end of the year he grew some more,
The loveliest dog you ever saw.
His coat was shiny, his bark was loud,
His tail kept wagging, though his eyes were sad.
He liked to run and chase his ball,
And loved his tummy rubs and all.

We went for walks both day and night,
To watch his joy was sheer delight.
With his nose down to the ground,
I'd watch him sniffing far around.
So many happy years we spent,
I have no idea where they went.
Before I knew it he was nine,
We'd been together for all that time.
Summer came, and then the Autumn,
And our walks began to shorten.
Winter came with its icy cold,
And I noticed he was getting old.
His body had stiffened just a bit,
But the springtime helped get rid of it.
We spent more time at home together,
Thinking it would last forever.
But time moves on which is so certain,
Came the day when he was 13.
His coat was grey, his eyes were dim,
His legs were going from under him.
As I hugged and kissed him so,
I knew he soon would have to go.
Eight weeks later my pal was gone,
He'd reached the end of his lifespan.
Before he went he licked my hand,
As if to say "I understand".

# Dog's Day

Three score and ten are given to man
But ours are a much briefer span
So though I give you all my heart
The time will come when we must part.

But all around you, you will see
Creatures that speak to you of me
A tired horse, a hunted thing
A sparrow with a broken wing…

Pity and help (I know you will)
And somehow I'll be with you still
And I shall know, although I'm gone
The love I gave you lingers on.

*Jane Anthony*

# Dachshund

A Dachshund's body is so long, he hasn't any notion,
How long it takes to tell his tail of his emotion.
So, when his eyes are filled with awful woe and sadness,
His tail goes wagging on because of previous gladness!

# Four Feet

I have done mostly what most men do
And pushed it out of my mind;
But I can't forget, if I wanted to,
Four feet trotting behind.

Day after day, the whole day through
Whenever my road inclined
Four feet said, I'm coming with you!
And trotted along behind

Now I must go by some other round
Which I shall never find
Somewhere that does not carry the sound
Of four feet trotting behind.

*Rudyard Kipling*

# Dedication For A Kennel

I love this little place because
It offers, after dark,
A pause for rest; A rest for paws;
A place to moor my bark.

# Dog Day

Nose-on-paws lies abask in the sun,
The task of the day not yet begun;
The cars to be chased, the delivery men
To be barked or wagged at now and again.

The cats to be filled with horrendous dread.
What cares, what labours lie still ahead;
So he must gather his vital force
To meet his duties to run his course.

Eight hours pass and the day is through,
With no more arduous tasks to do;
A buried bone in a garden bed,
A friendly hand on the leash he led.

Three cats chased and a ball to find
And new conviction that is man is kind.
Nose-on-paws, in the setting sun,
Rests in the glow of duties done.

*Dorothy Brown Thompson*

# Anniversary Thanks

Thank you so much for having me,
We have been so happy, haven't we?
God has promised that we will be,
Together again eventually.
One more lick and he closed his eyes,
We both had said our last goodbyes.
I can't describe the tears that fell,
The day he dies, I died as well.
Twelve months now I've been alone,
I've lost the doggie that I owned.
I sit and stare out into space,
And seem to see his lovely face.
I turn and look into the hall,
Where he used to run when he was small.
All around the memories stay,
They will until I'm called away.
Yes, I brought a puppy home one day,
It seems like only yesterday.
But it was 14 years today,
Since he first came with me to stay.

# The Seeing Eye

When I was but a little chap
My Mammy said to me
"When you grow up, darling Pup,
What would you like to be?"

"Oh, Mammy dear," I said to her,
"I saw a dog today,
Whose job was just the very thing,
I'd like in every way,

He walks besides a lady,
Whose eyes are void of light,
He leads her safely everywhere,
He is her guide, her sight.

Now here I am, dear people
Prepared and trained and fit,
Come, open wide your heart and hand,
And help me do my bit."

*William Tainsh*

# Whose Dog?

Who owns the dog you hear them say
Regarding the hound that is a stray,
Or has it been left unleashed
By its owner for the day.

Who owns the dog that barks and growls
In a small backyard with the fowls,
Out in the weather, no water or friends,
And the owner does not hear its howls.

Who owns the dog that slips its chain,
And jumps the low fence with distain,
To find somewhere it can relieve
Its thirst and loneliness pain.

Who owns the dog that roams the street,
And causes the motorists it chances to meet
To suddenly swerve with hasty stops,
Just missing the dog by a few feet.

Who owns the dog the pound receives
Where the sad hound for his master grieves,
Then the council charges and total costs
Are too much, the owner perceives.

Who owns the dog whose untimely death
That goes unnoticed, now without breath,
Lies unloved in an unmarked grave
With many others, buried beneath.

Who owns the dog that was a joy
On Christmas Day, a fluffy toy,
But when it grows to be a friend,
Its life a thoughtless owner will destroy.

Who owns the dog with devotion so deep
That keeps us safe while we soundly sleep,
Perhaps some awesome omnipotent Power
Has given the dog "our teachings" to keep.

So who owns the dog, a man's best friend
That cares for his master and will tend,
With year of love, and gladly die
At his feet, faithful to the end.

*Gordon Butterworth*

# The Dog Owners If

If you can curb your dog when all about you
Are losing theirs and couldn't give a damn,
If you can train him how to "come" and "sit" and "stay"
While others only run away and scram,
If you can keep him quiet, not too noisy
And wake your neighbours from their hard-earned sleep
If you can stop him jumping fences
And not rush out to snap at passing feet.

If you can keep him groomed, and wormed, and healthy
And see he gets his shots down at the vets
And make him sit beside you in the surgery,
And not take on a dozen other pets,
And in the winter sees his bed is draught free,
And sees he always gets enough to eat
And never let him fossick in the dustbins
That every Monday morning line your street.

If you can fill the unforgiving minute
With half an hour's walking on the lead
If you can keep him heeled and right beside you,
And not a threshing, withering fiend,
And when at night you settle with the paper
Into your usual warm and comfy chair,
Do you drop a loving hand to tell him
How happy you are knowing he is there.

And if when he is old, you love to help him
Face the cold, the aches, the ravages of time,
And with his life's a burden, not a pleasure
You'll help him to that other world sublime,
If you can say that all these rules you've followed
And have never shirked your duties to your dog,
Your life has been the richer for him,
And he has thought you … not a man, but God.

*Marcia Clarke*

# With Love, Together

We can look back now, you and I,
On quite a stretch of time gone by
Since, as a pup, I came to see
That you were all the world to me.

They haven't all been primrose ways.
That we have trodden since those days;
It hasn't all been sunny weather
That we have travelled through together.

But though the seasons come and go,
One faith remains, one thing I know;
Without you, life stands still and when
I hear your voice, I live again.

For years, though they can make us old,
Can never make the heart grow cold;
And youth that's fading has no sting
Where love is, time can't do a thing.

*Jane Anthony*

# My Dog

Who, if I plant a shrub or tree,
Engage it in a tugging spree
Plus a christening ceremony?

Who, if the washing's hanging low
Says to himself, "now ready, set, go"
And attacks it like a wild taureau?

Who scratches paint off all my doors
Demanding entrance with frantic paws
Woofing his head off just for encores?

Who sneaks snoozes on the settee
The chairs, med and consequently
The coat he sheds always clings to me?

Who, when the whole world seems askew,
Can I sit and tell my troubles to
And he understands my point of view?

Who, if I should arrive home late,
Waits for and welcomes me at the gate
No questionnaire to explicate?

Who, I know, if I were in strife
Would come to my aid mid dangers rife
And protect me with his very life?

Who, shows me so expressively
Each day by his love and loyalty
That to him I am a VIP?
My dog.

*Myrna Curtis*

# Twelve Years 'On The Chain'

I once was a frisky young puppy,
Disporting myself in the sun,
And rushing about with my brothers
From dawn until daylight was done.
We chased the wild birds in the bushes,
And chivvied the cats through the hay,
Barking and scrambling and pushing
In our top heavy, awkward way.

But a thing called a man got possession
Of me, the most lively of three;
My soft baby neck encircled
With a chain he made fast to a tree.
I tore at the chain and I whimpered,
I howled, but my howling was in vain,
For no mercy he knew, nor compassion
He felt, for a young creature's pain.

"He has water and food in abundance,
And a comfortable kennel" said he;
But oh how I hated the comforts!
I'd have bartered them all to be free,
Like the dogs on the farms round about us,
That worked while they worked and then played

And were wonderful pals to their owners –
Ah me! What a pal I'd have made.

But no palship for me, and no freedom.
I've been for 12 years on the chain;
I've grown old and ferocious and savage,
While guarding a bad master's gain.
But perhaps in the final accounting
When each shall be given his due,
The life of the creatures he's broken,
May be placed in the balances, too.

There is something out there in the shadows,
A something I just faintly see,
For my eyes are dimming and
    glazing
And all things seem distant to me
As it comes out and slowly
    advances,
Around me there falls a strange
    peace –
I should rush out and bite,
    but I cannot,
For that something – is
    bringing – release.

*H Barclay*

# With Love From A Lonely Dog

I wish someone would tell me,
What it is I've done wrong
Why do I have to stay chained up
And be left alone so long?

They seemed so glad to have me
When I came here as a pup.
There were so many things we'd do
While I was growing up.

The master said he'd train me
As a companion and a friend,
The mistress said she'd never fear
To be alone again.

The children said they'd feed me
And brush me every day,
They'd play with me and walk me
If I would only stay.

But now the master "hasn't time"
The mistress says "the shed"
She doesn't want me in the house
Not even to be fed.

The children never walk me
They always say "not now"
I wish that I could please them,
Won't someone tell me how?

All I had you see was love
I wish they would explain
They said they always wanted me
And then left me on a chain.

*Gwen Cresswell*


# Corgi

The corgi is of Welsh descent.
His ancestors in Wales
Rounded up the mountain sheep
By nipping at their tails.

Perhaps that is the reason why
The corgi's tail is clipped
Down to a tiny, rounded stub
So the nipper can't be nipped.

*Jim Killard*

# My Phantom Hand

I would not think those good brown eyes
Have lost their light of life so soon
But in some canine Paradise
Your wraith I know rebukes the moon,
And quarters every plain and hill
seeking his master. As for me,
The gods at least this prayer fulfil
That when I cross the flood and see
Old Charron on the Stygian coast
Take toll of all the shades that land,
Your little, faithful breaking ghost
Will leap to lick my phantom hand.

# Chihuahua

The Chihuahua is so very small
He almost isn't there at all,
But watch him in a fight
Attacking victims from beneath
Those snapping, needle-pointed teeth
Inflict a painful bite.

*Jim Killard*


# I Had A Little Dog Called Spot

I had a little dog called Spot,
I put him in a bath that was much too hot.
He drank all the water, and ate all the soap,
I took him to the doctor's, but the doctor said "No hope".

# Dogs

I'd like to be a dog you know, sniffing around the town
Nose around a bit of white or around a bit of brown.
I'd love to bark at traffic and lift me leg on tyres
And send black cats up telephone poles and out
    along the wires.

I'd love the double-jointedness of reaching all me bits
And never care where I aim or what I miss or hits
I'd love to have me belly rubbed till me back legs
    start reacting
And sow me oats all down the street with no thought
    of prophylactin!

I'd curl up on the bedspread when no one else
    was looking,
I'd hang around the table and pick up bits of cooking
I'd love to have me little fluffs blamed upon the kids,
And wake up half the neighbourhood by banging
    dirt bin lids.

A dog's life is as cushy as a creatures life could get,
'Cept I'd hate it if my favourite parts were lopped
    off by the vet!

# Our Dog's Gone Bananas

My father found this mongrel dog,
We called the thing Banana;
Each Sunday night it used to pound,
Upon our grand piarna.

And with no word of instruction,
It would grab the violin;
Give a three-bar introduction,
And then we'd all pile in.

Dad reckoned with a dog so smart,
He would donate some time to train it;
But the mongrel almost broke his heart,
I thought that he might brain it.

As Grandma suffered fading sight,
When father trained the hound;
To show her round the town at night,
They would finish in the pound.

Ma said each time it took Gran out,
Be home early should the fog start;
You take my word, without a doubt,
They would come home in the dog cart.

At a weekly get-together,
We all kicked up a stink;
As a vote was taken whether,
We should down it in the drink.

All spoke against this line of thought,
A secret vote was taken;
In favour numbered 10 to nought,
A recount proved this not mistaken.

My father sang, "Goodbye my Love",
And we all joined in the chorus;
Perhaps we'll all meet up above,
But the dog got home before us.

There are many stories handed down,
But the one that I like most;
Is the Sunday we came tired from town,
And it took off with the roast.

From the wall Mum grabbed the chopper,
Where for 50 years was rusting;
Me father tried to stop 'er,
Their language was disgusting.

Round the house they all went hunting,
Me Mum, the dog, the meat;
Our show prize pig was grunting,
Then some dogs from up the street.

They disappeared into the night,
We had tea and forgot 'em;
When next they all appeared in sight,
I believe the Mayor just shot 'em.

Somehow I miss that mongrel dog,
We never got another;
I also miss our show prize hog,
Sometimes I miss me mother.

*Bill Handley*

# My Doggie

I have a little doggie
Who used to sit and beg,
Doggie stumbled down the stairs
And broke his little leg.

Oh doggie I will nurse you
Try to make you well,
You will have a collar on
With a little bell.

When your leg is better
We will run and play,
We shall scamper round the fields
And watch them making hay.

*Caroline Roberts*

# Dachshund

From east to west and west to east
The dachshund is a lengthy beast.
From north to south he's stubby.
When through the mud he runs around
His under carriage, close to ground,
Becomes extremely grubby.

*Jim Killard*

# Growing Up Lament

Please love me as you used to,
The way I still love you,
I promise I won't eat too much,
Or do, what I shouldn't do.
I'll bark, only if I should bark,
Whenever strangers call
And I'll try so hard to please you,
For I want and need you all.
You were so delighted with me
A few short months ago,
But now you say I'm a problem
And I will have to go.

Please love me as you used to,
When I was a cute pup,
I haven't changed so very much,
Except to just grow up.

Doesn't everybody do that,
I'm sure you once were small
And other than to grow in size
No, I haven't changed at all.
I'm still "me", as I will always be,
Don't leave me here this way,
Please, take me home again with you,
You know I'm not a "stray".

Please love me as you used to.

*Myrna Curtis*

*The town was Warrensburg, Missouri; the year, 1870. A dog owner was suing another townsman who had shot his dog, and was asking $50 damages. The crowd in the Court sat hushed as Lawyer George Graham Vest, representing the dog owner, made his final plea. When he had finished, the jury retired to return within minutes with its verdict. The award? Not the $50 the owner had asked – but $500! This is Senator Vest's tribute to "man's best friend".*

# The Noble Dog

The best friend that a man may have in the world may turn against him and become his enemy. The son or daughter he has reared with loving care may prove ungrateful. Those who are nearest and dearest, those whom we trust with our happiness and our good name may become traitors to their faith.

The money that a man has he may lose. It flies away from him, perhaps when he needs it most. A man's reputation may be sacrificed in a moment of ill-considered action.

The people who are prone to fall upon their knees to do us honour when success is with us may be the first to throw the stone of malice when failure settles its clouds upon our heads.

The one absolutely unselfish friend that a man can have in this selfish world, is one that never deserts him, the one that never proves ungrateful or treacherous, is his dog.

A man's dog stands by him in prosperity and poverty, in health and in sickness. He will sleep on the cold ground, where the wintry winds blow and the snow drives fiercely, if only he may be near his master's side.

He will kiss the hand that has no food to offer; he will lick the wounds and sores that come in encounters and roughness of the world. He guards the sleep of his pauper master as if he were a prince. When all other friends desert, he remains. When riches take wings and reputation falls to pieces, he is as constant in his love as the sun in its journey through the heavens.

If fortune drives the master forth, an outcast in the world, friendless and homeless, the faithful dog will go with him. And when the last scene of all comes – no matter if all other friends pursue their way – there will the noble dog be found; his head between his paws, his eyes sad but open in alert watchfulness, faithful and true – even in death.

# The Complaint Of A Trained Dog

Moping in the pleasant sun
I ask, what is it I have done
That I am kept a prisoner here,
Chained to my kennel through the year?
I do my duty night and day
By warning wicked men away;
My master's house I closely guard,
While he sleeps safe – yet my reward
Is to be treated like a thief
To me no season brings relief.

They send the children out to play,
To stretch their little legs they say;
But the poor dog – who thinks of him?
He longs to use each stiffening limb.
I hear the schoolboys howl and run;
How I could help them in their fun!
And when I now and then obtain
A half-hour's freedom from my chain
I am so nearly mad with joy,
I am as bad as any boy.

But if I had an hour each day
For healthful exercise and play,
I could be sober as a judge.
Strange that my master still should grudge
The little trouble it would be
To give so great a boon to me.
'Tis true I often hear him say
I'm a good house-dog – but I pray
To have – instead of empty praise –
Freedom to brighten these long days.
How I do wish that he could be
For one whole week chained up like me;
Some pity then might reach his mind.
If fellow feeling makes us kind,
Master! you know I am true
And faithful servant still to you;
I earn my wages – pay them me –
They are not gold but liberty.

# Spotty's Christmas

Spotty was a mongrel pup who didn't have a home;
A cruel master cast him out upon the streets to roam.
The air was cold, the snow lay thick, no meal did he receive,
Or cheer to tide him on his way, and it was Christmas Eve.

He'd hunted alley-ways and streets for food of any kind,
And tried a rubbish bin or two but nothing he could find.
And now, as ev'ning shadows fell he heaved a mournful sigh,
And sniffed the fragrant cooking from the cottages nearby.

His little ribs were poking out; his frame was gaunt and thin,
And where his matted haunch arose, his tummy tumbled in.
Ah me! It was a dreadful state of puppy-dog affairs,
But Spotty was too brave, you know, to think of shedding tears.

Although he knew starvation loomed, and that his end was near,
He tried to jump and bark a bit, pretending not to care.
There lay across his tragic path a house of pomp and fame,
Where wealthy folk in carriages and lavish raiment came.

As peeping from the window still he spied the luscious drops
Of gravy, on a roasted duck, he licked his hungry chops.
Then from his nose a quiver rose and travelled to his tail;
Such sights as these, such ecstasies, made staunchest
    courage fail.

So to the door he boldly went, and barked in hopeful strain
Until a poodle dog came out, who eyed him with disdain.
"What do you want? You ragged dog," she snapped
    contemptuously,
"And who gave you permission, sir, to come disturbing me.
Be quick and state your business now, and say what
    you're about,
Or sure as fate I'll call the house and have you bundled out."

"Oh, please!" gasped Spot, "I'm hungry, ma'am. Tis shelter
    that I seek,
And you have much to offer here, to one who's starved
    and weak."
"Indeed I have," the poodle barked, "and virtue's shining way,
Has brought this very just reward; I'm not a useless stray.
If you had plied your wits to work and planned your
    conduct well,
You, too, would have a home tonight and different tale to tell."

She slammed the door and went her way, with scornful
    nose held high,
And left poor Spotty on the step, to faint away or die.
Injustice bowed his spirit down, and cruel insult hurled,
Upon his stainless character, from out a wicked world.

                                          continued over page...

His little heart was beating fast; his brain was reeling round;
He struggled bravely on a pace, then tumbled to the ground.
But through the misty eventide there came an angel fair,
Who stopped and knelt at Spotty's side and gazed upon
    him there.
He had not wings, nor harp of gold, nor shining halo bright;
Just gentle arms and tender heart, that understood his plight.
And so he picked him up and wrapped him warm within his coat,
And vainly tried to quell the lump that rose within his throat.

And Spotty opened weary eyes and showed, as doggies can
His joy, and licked the fingers of a strange and kindly man.
Then neither spoke or made a sound, as though they
    knew of yore
A miracle at Christmas time had happened once before.

This story ends in glad refrain, with little left to tell;
Spot found a home, a kindly friend, and lots to eat as well,
On Christmas Day, I'm pleased to say, he barked in
    rapturous tones,
Because, beside his bed, he found a stocking full of bones.

# Pekinese

Pekinese
Come in hes and shes
But because they wear
Woolly mops of hair,
It's hard to tell for certain
(Behind that hairy curtain)
Which are hes
And which are shes.
It's just as well
That Pekinese can tell
The difference

*Jim Killard*

# My Dog - Before And After

I am in darkness, nowhere to hide
The sounds and vibrations what's outside
Weeks go by, maybe I will be the strain, the pride
Day has come; my nails will be clipped and nipped
Something I cannot hide from nor confide.
Stand tall, be counted, I am not wild
I love so dearly to be by someone's side,
Not truly for confrontation, to help and guide
To be there when no one cares if I live or die.
Follow me true friend, I cannot tell a lie
The best of years I will show in your eyes.

# The Empty Kennel

Our yard is quiet, his kennel's empty now,
My friends boast dog, proud, pedigreed and bigger.
But hair will whiten, care will crease this brow
Before I find another dog like Digger…

A little ginger mongrel? Aye that's all,
But Ah … he won my heart in countless ways.
Will new eyes speak such love, new pals recall
Our rambles on those sunny Saturdays.

He left me in the first, pale light of dawn
He left me … but he does not leave forever.
For on some brighter day he'll wake and yawn,
"Good morning God", and then no time will sever…

I wrap him in my best silk scarf, I kneel.
These hands that patted, press the final sod,
I cannot weep, bewildered, lost, I feel
A "god" bereaved, yet nearer to my GOD.

*Louis Clark*

# The Dog
# (As Seen By The Cat)

The dog is black or white or brown,
And sometimes spotted like a clown.
He loves to make a foolish noise,
And human company he enjoys.

The human people pat his head
And teach him to pretend he's dead,
And beg, and fetch, and carry too;
Things that no well-bred cat will do.

At human jokes, however stale,
He jumps about and wags his tale,
And human people clap their hands
And think he really understands.

They say "Good Dog" to him. To us
They say "Poor Puss", and make no fuss.
Why dogs are good and cats are "poor"
I fail to understand, I'm sure.

To someone very good and just,
Who has proved worthy of her trust,
A cat will sometimes condescend –
The dog is everybody's friend!

*Oliver Herford*

# The Power Of The Dog

There is sorrow enough in the natural way
From men and women to fill our day;
But when we are certain of sorrow in store,
Why do we always arrange for more?
Brothers and sisters, I bid you beware
Of giving your heart to a dog to tear.

Buy a pup and your money will buy
Love unflinching that cannot lie
Perfect passion and worship fed
By a kick in the ribs, or a pat on the head.
Nevertheless, it is hardly fair
To risk your heart for a dog to tear.

When the 14 years which nature permits
Are closing in asthma, or tumour, or fits,
And the vet's unspoken prescription runs,
To lethal chambers or loaded guns
Then you will find – it's your own affair
But … you've given your heart to a dog to tear.

When the body that lived at you single will,
When the whimper of welcome is still (how still!)
When the spirit that answered your every mood
Is gone – wherever it goes – for good
You will discover how much you care,
And will give your heart to a dog to tear.

We've sorrow enough in the natural way,
when it comes to buying Christian clay,
Our loves are not given but only lent
At compound interest of cent per cent.
Though it's not always the case, I believe
That the longer we've kept 'em, the more we do grieve
For when doubts are payable, right or wrong,
A short-time loan is as bad as long –
So why in heaven (before we are there)
Should we give our hearts to a dog to tear?

*Rudyard Kipling*

# Goodbye

Kip has left us –
Gone to that last great lamp post in the sky,
Where all true city dogs aspire to go
When they die.

He's happy there –
Young, alert and vigorous enough again
To follow trails with frenzied expectation
Released from pain.

The house is hollow –
Echoing with the sound of joyous bark
At mention of the daily, shared excursion
To the park.

Soulful eyes –
Stare upward, hopefully, at every bite we eat.
A small, brown form lies, log-like, by the fire
At our feet.

A hazy shadow –
Hovers by the empty bowl upon the floor.
Scampering paws along the hall bid welcome
At the door.

All sad illusions –
But, through the silent, gathering mist of tears,
Shine the thoughts and happy memories
Of 14 years.

*Judie Hillard*

A dog has lots of friends
Because he wags
His tail and not his tongue

# An Honoured Place

So many things at times the heart do sear,
With pain; and cause us sad, unhappy goad,
And one such thing that hurts me so – to hear
My old brown friend has passed on down that road,
From which no mortal creatures 'ere return.
Us creatures all of flesh and bone and blood,
Some day will all surely have our turn,
When we will too return to clay and mud.
So you, old Shep, old friend and pal so fine,
Who shared our lives, whose back was strong and loud,
It kept us safe from all – I hope you shine
Among the stars; and happily endowed
With spirit free, and trusting dear old face
In memories, you've earned your honoured place.

*Denton Pratt*

# Is There A Dog Heaven?

In my quiet moments I wonder
Is there a dog heaven up yonder?
I'd like to think that one day I'll see
The pets who meant so much to me.
They weren't like humans – full of greed.
So, when from this earthly life they're freed
I'm sure that God with a loving Hand
Strokes each head. For surely He planned
That creatures with hearts so full of love
Will reap their reward up above.

Do they trot behind God at a pace,
Wagging their tails – a grin on their face,
The same as they did with us here on earth?
I wonder if we appreciated their worth.

In my quiet moments I fancy I see
My pets running to greet me.
They'll lick my face, they'll lick my hand,
This ever-faithful loving band,
And I will know I'm home at last
With my Maker and my pets from the past.

*Joan de Nijs*

# Short And Sweet

Our little dog fell off the roof,
After eating Christmas pud.
I threw it in the rubbish bin,
Because it was no good.

You see, its leg was broken,
And my Mother always said,
It's cheaper than to get things fixed,
To buy new ones instead.

*Bill Handley*

# A Little Stray

I am a little stray that's lost
Wanting a good home at any cost,
Please come and set me free
Or put me out of my misery.
I am as affectionate as can be,
With lots of love to give to thee
I have lots of friends you see
That are in the same position as me.
All we want is a chance to be
In a loving family.
Please come and collect me and
I will be as happy as can be.

*Diane Rogers*

# Scruffy – In Memory Of

Dig the earth and dig it deep
Let him rest and let him sleep.
He was loyalty and trust,
Gone, as we must go, to dust.

Faithful eyes that watch your own,
Ears that cocked for every tone
Looks that told us every day
Love that humans seldom pay.

Dull, or fearful, tasks to do,
Still his footsteps followed you.
Just a dog – but what a plan!
Given as a friend to man!

Dig the earth and dig it deep
Let him rest and let him sleep.
God who knows that hearts can break
Sent him here to share that ache.

*W Rubiek*

# If It Should Be...

If it be I grow frail and weak,
And pain should wake me from my sleep,
Then you must do what must be done,
For this last battle can't be won.

You will be sad – I understand
Don't let your grief then stay your hand.
For this day, more than all the rest,
Your love and friendship stand the test.

We've had so many happy years,
What is to come will hold no fears.
You'd not want me to suffer … so
When the time comes, please let me go.

Take me where all my needs they'll tend,
But stay with me until the end.
And hold me firm and speak to me
Until my eyes no longer see.

I know in time you too will see,
It is a kindness you do to me.
Although my tail its last has waved,
From pain and suffering I've been saved.

Do not grieve that it should be you
Who must decide this thing to do.
We've been so close – we two – these years,
Don't let your heart hold any tears.

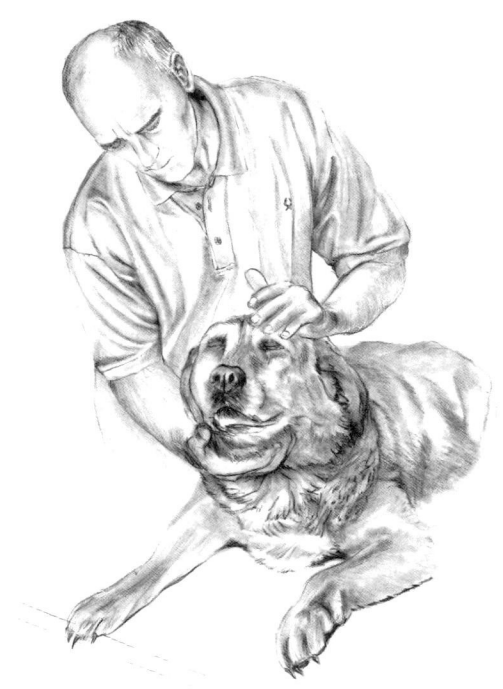

# The White Dog

A little white puppy sat all alone;
In a rather small cage in a shop,
And as I was passing he whimpered at me,
And his eyes seemed to beg me to stop.
And I pulled Mother's hand and I whispered and said
"Please, will you wait while I just pat his head?"

He was such a soft little fat, furry thing,
And his eyes were so shiny and bright.
I pulled his brown ears and tickled his neck,
And he gave me little squeals of delight.
And his tiny pink tongue popped out quicker than quick,
And curled round my finger and gave it a lick.

He scratched with his paws at the bars of his cage,
And I felt that I just couldn't bear
To leave him alone in a cage any more –
He did look so sorrowful there.
And he pawed at my hand with a sad little whine,
And I whispered to Mother, "I wish he were mine".

It seemed very cruel for us both to go home
When he wanted to come with us too
And we stayed and we stayed till at last Mother said:
"I suppose I must buy him for you!"
And a man came and got him and gave him to me,
And he licked me all over as glad as could be.

*Christine Bradley*

# Nearly Home

Swift as a lion and just as strong, he sped toward that place
Where one bright night he'd made sweet love, beyond a
    long, sweet chase
Although, just once before,
And he was big and he was strong,
Was Brent, the Labrador.

And just as swift and just as keen, as hearing
    sounds he knew,
He thought it time for better things and so t'ward
    home he flew,
So well he knew this pleasure, as nearly home he tore
And he was big and black and strong,
Was Brent, the Labrador.

But much more swift and much more strong, the great
    iron monster came,
The loving creature only heard his mistress call his name.
And so he ran, and so he died, it wasn't long before,
and he was big but not that strong,
Was Brent, the Labrador.

As clear as light and just as real, we feel his loving trust,
And I for one know without doubt, that Brent's not
    only dust.
With him we'd known such pleasure we'd never
    known before,
Yes, he was big and strong and ours,
Was Brent, the Labrador.

# Bella

All hail my small, four-footed friend
Your wistful eyes a message send,
A ball to catch, a shoe to chew
That's all a small Bella asks of you.

Except perhaps a friendly word
A touch of fun to chase a bird,
All day my small, four-footed friend
On longing hope she does depend.

Not asking much she wags her tail
Never a whimper or a wail,
But joyous greeting Bella sends
With quivering nose greets any friend
Who spares the time to pat her head
And see that she at last is fed.

*Evelyn McGill*

## Boxer

A good boxer never dies, he always stays,
And walks beside you on crisp autumn days,
When frost is on the fields and when the year
Is ending and the winter's drawing near.
And when it's summer and when the bees are humming
He leaps ahead of you and awaits your coming,
And anytime you're lonely, look, you'll see
His great eyes watching you solemnly.
Just call him in your heart, he'll cease his play
His head within your hand in his old way.

# Brandy

Brown eyes so soft had she
Gentle paw upon my knee,
Mouth that laughed with eager glee
As she greeted her mistress – me.

Faithful friend, never glum
Always ready for a little fun,
Chasing ball or chasing me
Then eagerly into tea.

When she first was mine
She and I were young and fair,
My troubles faithful Brandy shared
When I needed her, always there.

Seventeen years of life she shared with me
Now rests in peace, her friendly face
No longer livens up the place
But the richness that her company brought
Will never be by me forgot

Sleep, Dear Brandy

*Evelyn Mcgill*

# A Poem For Dog Lovers

Outside the pearly gates, they wait above the stars,
Watching with eager wistful eyes behind the golden bars,
Hoping the man they loved on earth, or the little
    boy who died,
May wander to the gates and pat the little heads outside.

I do not think that I could rest behind the gates of gold,
Knowing those faithful loving hearts were waiting
    in the cold,
And so, when comes the call for me to cross the
    great divide,
I hope the Lord will let me have a little place outside.

*Jill Evans*

# The Earl Of Ascot

Ascot came to live with us
in the winter of '79,
A quiet dog, no mess no fuss
and he didn't bark or whine…

He was six months' old and nearly grown
and he soon settled in for the better,
But it wasn't long before we were shown
how to live with a big Red Setter…

He showered us with affection,
and he tried to sit on our knee,
For his heart couldn't take rejection,
the hurt in his eyes you could see…

But he soon took over the household
Had us all at his beck and call,
As time went by, he became more bold
And was the biggest Red Devil of all…

He chewed everything he could find in the place,
And a sock was his special delight,
If you chased him he'd wait till you were face to face
Then take off like a bird in flight…

Well, things have sure changed since Ascot arrived
As for love, he just couldn't give more,
Most of the traumas so far, we've survived
And it's worth it to just shake his paw…

*Elaine Fairbairn*

# Sally Dog

She sits and waits right near the door
Or lies around all over the floor,
A little "Woof", can I come in?
After all, I'm really kin.

Then waddle waddle skippily hop
She'll follow you round then just drop.
She doesn't get round as best she did
After all she's sure no kid.

Can't go for a walk or even a job
Just a grand old lab called Sally Dog.

*Rob Clark*

# Lady

She's chubby and fat
This dog of mine,
But her figure sure
To me is fine.

A cattle dog
With no cattle to chase,
Far too many kilos
To keep up the pace.

Steals for herself
Any bones left around,
Then barks to say
Hi, look what I've found.

Almost human
This lady of mine,
Though I growl a lot
She really is fine.

I'm sure she understands
My thoughts and love,
Settled in her chair
Like a turtle dove.

She ponders and dreams
In thoughts like mine,
As sleepiness robs
Her mind of time.

*Bob Duddy and Joe Burke*

# Fleur

She had such spirit and so many charms,
This little dog that sleeps in my arms,
I love her dark eyes that can look so forlorn,
I have cared for her from the day she was born.

Together we fought so that she might live,
This little dog that had so much to give.
There were dark times when she struggled for breath,
I couldn't give up, it would have meant her death.

Time has passed and now she's two years old,
Thoroughly spoilt, never does as she is told.
It gives me great joy to see her each day
Enjoying her life, whether at sleep or at play.

My other dog Cuddles taught Fleur to play rough
Then came the times when I shouted "Enough!!"
Fleur looks around at me in surprise,
"Mum, you know I can do no wrong in your eyes,
Cuddles and I are just having fun you know",
I give a laugh and off they go.

It's all over now, my Fleur is gone
We were together just over 10 years,
Her heart gave out, it could take no more,
All I have now are memories and my tears.

*Beryl Barrett*

# A Piddling Pup

A farmer's dog once came to town
His Christian name was Pete,
He had a pedigree two yards long
And his looks were hard to beat.

And as he trotted down the street
T'was wonderful to see,
His work on every corner
His work on every tree.

The city still stood looking on
With deep and jealous rage,
To see a simple country dog
The piddler of the age.

Then, to show the city dogs
That he didn't give a damn,
Walked straight into the grocer's shop
And piddled on the ham.

He piddled on the onions
And he piddled on the floor,
And when the grocer kicked him out
He piddled on the door.

Then all the dogs from far and wide
Were summoned with a yell,
To sniff the country stranger off
And fudge him with their smell.

They sniffed beneath his stumpy tail
Their praise for him ran high,
But when one did sniff underneath
Pete piddled in his eye.

Then all the dogs knew what they'd do
They'd start a piddling carnival
And see the stranger through.

But on and on when noble Pete
To piddle on every standhill,
Till all the city champions
Were piddled to a standstill.

Then noble Pete an exhibition gave
Of all the ways to piddle,
Like fancy flips and double drips
And now and then a dribble.
Then finally the city dogs said
"So long friend
In piddling you did defeat us"
But no one ever put them wise
That Pete had diabetes.

# A Wag Of A Tale

What do you call a dog? Well, I thought of Rover, Towser, and a dozen other names, but finally decided to settle for something a little different, I called my dog "sex". I was very young and didn't see the problems. One day I took "sex" for a walk, and he ran away from me. I spent hours looking for that dog. A policeman came along and asked me what I was doing in the alley at 4am in the morning. I said I was looking for "sex". He cautioned me that I should control my lust and that, if I was seen again, he would book me. I hurried off amused that he thought my dog was called "lust".

Later I had to get a dog licence for "sex". I asked the clerk for a licence for "sex"; he said he would like one too. I told him that it was for a dog, and he said the poor girl probably couldn't help what she looked like. I said: "You don't understand; I've had 'sex' since I was nine." He looked me up and down and remarked: "By the look of you I would not be surprised."

When I decided to get married, I told the minister that I wanted to have "sex" at the wedding. He said it was customary to wait until after the ceremony. I insisted that "sex" had played a major role in my life, in fact my whole life to this point had revolved around "sex". He said he didn't want to hear about my personal hang-ups, and that I should find somewhere more appropriate to get married. "Well," I said, "everyone coming to the wedding would enjoy having 'sex' there." He mumbled something about my ancestry, suggested my parents may not have been married at the time of my birth, and recommended a specialist he knew. We got married at a registry office, and they would not allow "sex" there either. We did have "sex" on our honeymoon though. I told the clerk at the hotel that we wanted a room for my wife and myself and a room for "sex". He said we were welcome to have "sex" in our own room and seemed confused when I told him it could be a little unhygienic. Anyway I told him, "sex" keeps us awake at night, and he said, yes, me too.

Then we separated, and sought a divorce. My wife wanted the dog. I said: "Your honour, I had 'sex' before we were married," and the Judge said: "Yes, me too." I told him the whole story, how after the married "sex" left us, he said yes, me too. Later the dog died. It was too much for me and I went to pieces. I had to see a psychiatrist, and she asked me: "What seems to be the trouble." I replied: "Well, 'sex' has died and left me. It's like losing a good friend and it's so lonely." The doctor looked at me and said: "Mister, you seem overly occupied with the thought of 'sex', it's not good for you, I know what you need … Get yourself a dog!"

# Last Will And Testament Of A Dog

"A 14-year-old dog died here, leaving an estate of $30,000. The money has been left to his owner and will now go for the care of other dogs."

Being of sound mind, as dogs go, which is sounder than some humans, I hereby declare this to be my last will and testament. I name no trustees or executors – as a dog has too much faith and confidence in the honesty and good will of the human race to consider any special provisions of this nature necessary. I disturb nobody. I am not beset by suspicions.

I do not request that all my just debts be paid.

Being a dog, I have never run into debt, and have always tried fully to return my obligations in love, devotion and protection, with compound interest.

I have, it is true, torn the fringe from a rug or two, scratched a few doors, and dug holes in the lawn. If anyone feels he should be remunerated, all very well, but it is my impression I was always detected, admonished and made to settle at the time. Money puzzles me. It has given me certain comforts and protection, but it can't be too good a factor in life because I have heard too many humans quarrel over it, and I am sure I would rather not know too much about it.

Having made these observations, I make these provisions:

1. To such dogs as are sick and in need I leave my entire estate, without specifying to the last comma just how this shall be done. It seems to me, being merely of canine intelligence, that something has to be left to good faith.

2. To my master and mistress I leave my undying love and devotion. I wish I had more to give. If there is a dog heaven, I hope to look upon them from there, hear their voices and catch something dearer to me than all the money on earth — the sound of their footsteps on gravel path.

By this hand and seal this 14th day of March 1944.

Codicils: None whatever. Dogs don't waver in their affections enough to require last-minute changes.

H. I Phillips
copied from the "Animals," the journal of the RSPCA (NSW).

# A Dog's Plea

Treat me kindly my beloved friend for no heart in all the world is more grateful for kindness than the loving heart of me.

Do not break my spirit with a stick for though I should lick your hand between blows, your patience and understanding will more quickly teach me the things you will have me learn. I may not always be right but I am always willing to forgive and be forgiven.

Speak to me often for your voice is the world's sweetest music, as you must know by the fierce wagging of my tail when your footsteps fall upon my waiting ear.

Please take me inside when it is cold and wet for I am a domesticated animal, no longer accustomed to rain, cold and bitter elements. I ask no greater glory than to have the privilege of sitting at your feet beside the hearth.

Keep my pan filled with fresh water, for I can not tell you when I suffer thirst. Feed me food that I may stay well, to romp and play and do your bidding. To walk by your side and stand ready, willing and able to protect you with my life, should your life be in danger.

I cannot tell you when I need medical care, or when injections are due, watch my movements and see if I am listless, shying away from food and take me to our friend the Veterinarian for a check-up on a regular basis.

And my friend when I am old, and no longer enjoy good health, hearing and sight, do not make heroic efforts to keep me going. I am not having any fun. Please see that my trusting life is taken gently.

I shall leave this earth knowing with the last breath I draw, that my fate was always safest in my hands.

All I ask is, stay with me until the need, hold me firm and speak to me until my ears no longer hear and my eyes no longer see.

*??? Manning*

# Choc the Water Spaniel

A brown water spaniel was racing
With glee through the bushes and heather.
He rushed through the valleys and dales
All other fast runners outpacing!
For we were exploring together
The beautiful scenes of North Wales.

With him as companion we wandered,
My father and I, and could witness
The speed of our swift canine friend.
He paused for a moment and pondered –
Then on! His exuberance and fitness
Unbounded seemed never to end!

One word would provoke a reaction –
We spoke of a *walk!* He would listen,
Ears cocked, and was keen to depart.
This thought had a magic attraction:
His eyes, bright and liquid, would glisten,
He barked and would urge us to start!

Once, seeking a fresh expedition,
He simply was *not* to be thwarted.
His lead in my right hand he pressed,
Then sat up and begged! his petition
Soon led to his being escorted
Once more with enjoyment and zest!

Old Choc was a notable figure
Possessing remarkable features:
His bark and his cute, floppy ears,
His tireless, unquenchable vigour,
which made him the rarest of creatures,
Still live in my mind through the years!

*Gilbert H. Brown*

# I Died Today

Dear Mum and Dad,

I died today. You got tired of me and took me to the shelter. They were overcrowded and I drew an unlucky number. I am in a plastic bag in a landfill now.

Some other puppy will get the barely used leash you left. My collar was dirty and too small. But the lady took it off before she sent me to Rainbow Bridge.

Would I still be at home if I hadn't chewed your shoe? I didn't know what it was, but it was leather, and it was on the floor. I was just playing. You forgot to get puppy toys.

Would I still be at home if I had been house broken? Rubbing my nose in what I did only made me ashamed that I had to go at all. There are books and obedience teachers that would have taught you how to teach me to go to the door.

Would I still be at home if I hadn't barked? I was only saying "I'm scared, I'm lonely, I'm here, I'm here! I want to be your best friend."

Would I still be at home if you had taken the time to care for me and to teach manners to me? You didn't pay attention to me after the first week or so, but I spent all my time waiting for you to love me. I died today.

Love,
Your Puppy.

# Message From a Little Ghost

I've explained to Saint Peter I'd rather stay here
Outside of the pearly Gate,
I wont be a nuisance, I wont even bark
I'll be very patient — and wait.

I'll lie here and chew a celestial bone
No matter how long you may be.
I miss you so much — if I went alone
It wouldn't be Heaven for me.

*Muriel Whitehead Jarvis*

# Rainbow Bridge

Just this side of heaven is a place called Rainbow Bridge. When an animal dies that has been especially close to someone here, that pet goes to Rainbow Bridge. There are meadows and hills for all our special friends so they can run and play together. There is plenty of food, water, and sunshine and our friends are warm and comfortable.

All the animals who have been ill and old are restored to health and vigour; those who were hurt or maimed are made whole and strong again, just as we remember them in our dreams of days and times gone by. The animals are happy and content, except for one small thing; they miss someone very special to them, who had to be left behind. They all run and play together, but the day comes when one suddenly stops and looks into the distance. His bright eyes are intent; his eager body begins to quiver. Suddenly, he begins to run from the group, flying over the green grass, his legs carrying him faster and faster.

You have been spotted, and when you and your special friend finally meet, you cling together in joyous reunion, never to be parted again. The happy kisses rain upon your face; your hands again caress the beloved head, and you look once more into the trusting eyes of your pet, so long gone from your life but never absent from your heart.

Then you cross Rainbow Bridge together…

# My Visit To The Surgery

I am sorry I growled at Julie, when I first came in,
My weight was down to 5.6; I must be getting thin,
I did let Alice pat me and Karen sneaked a cuddle,
I thought I was very good, didn't even struggle.

Kylie put a collar on me and gave me my pre med.
While my Mum was hanging on to me around my little head.
My Mum said when she left that "here I had to stay"
The next I know I'm on my own for the whole of the day,
And later I discovered it was all night too,
Who made that decision to remove my fangs, Austin, was it you?

Now I have hardly any maulers so I cant bite you anymore,
The next time I visit, the muzzle stays in the drawer.
I really have to ask you, now you have taken my teeth,
"How am I to chew on bones or on a piece of beef"?
"And where will the Doggie Tooth Fairy go when she comes from Heaven
To collect and leave lots of money for all of my ELEVEN"?
Eleven! You took eleven! Eleven of my best,
Now I only have three, which are not many left.

I want to sincerely thank you for looking after me,
For taking me out this morning so I could do a pee,
I did have a lot of trouble trying to find a tree,
Or one that I could recognise was difficult to see.

My Mum and Dad picked me up to take me back home,
I've been to the beach several times so I could have a
    roam,
My mouth is feeling better; I'm taking the prescribed pills,
And trying to chase the Postman when he leaves the bills,
I'm eating special food that my Mum prepares you see,
I'm glad that I am home, my Mum and Dad love me.

*From Jack the toothless terroriser, written by his Mum, Gail Cox.*

# Ode to Angus

Eleven years we had him
Our great little mate
Black eyes – pricked ears – and a tail so straight
A more sincere friend
You could never meet
Always there with you, or curled up at your feet
He was just so special
He could all but talk
It was amazing the way he'd con you into a walk
Just down to the park
It would make his day
For the joy that he gave us – a small price to pay
A tap on the shoulder
Asked to join you in bed
A nudge on the leg said, "time to be fed!"
If you were down
He could cheer you up
Grab a ball or a toy, and carry on like a pup

His face at the window
Waiting for you to come home
Would make you feel guilty, leaving him there all alone
But the day that you'd had
Would seem better by a mile
When he'd bounce out to greet you with a fair dinkum smile
With the kids – at cricket
Or camping we shared
Some wonderful times with the pup that we reared
But now it's St. Peter
He greets at the gate
For your life – and our memories, we're grateful
Thanks mate!

*Bill & Joan & Justin & Sally – Anne Sargood*

# Pal Of Mine

Since I've known him he's been by my side,
Maybe early maybe late at night,
he looks at me and I can see
he's a pal of mine.

People may forsake me,
fate may be unkind,
But in all the worlds truer friend
you'll never find.

When I'm sad and I need company,
he wags his tail and so he comforts me,
I pat his head and take him to bed,
he's a pal of mine.

*John Moore*

# The Devotion of Greyfriars Bobby

Greyfriars Churchyard! Hallowed ground
where historic graves abound –
Home of Scotland's honoured dead!
Many years have passed and fled
Since in this secluded spot,
By historians ne'er forgot,
true devotion was displayed
By a faithful dog who stayed
By his master's grave on guard,
Braving winters cold and hard.

Once a farmer named John Gray
Every week on market-day
Came to Edinburgh, where
Business he transacted. There
Tasks important he completed
And for a host of farmers greeted.
or he was, across the years,
Called "Auld Jock" among his peers.
No one heartier seemed or merrier,
And he owned a small Skye terrier
Who, devoted and content,
Followed him where'er he went.
When the castle's booming gun
Sounded out the hour of one,
Dog and master would repair
To a neighbouring restaurant, where

The proprietor, John Traill,
Would provide them without fail
With the sustenance they needed.
Touchingly the terrier pleaded —
Then his unusual bun would claim
Proudly. Bobby was his name.

When auld Jock this life departed
Bobby fretted, broken hearted:
'Twas for him a dire disaster,
For he dearly loved his master,
Who, when last respects were paid,
Was in Greyfriars Churchyard laid.
Faithful Bobby was the chief
Mourner — he was filled with grief
and supreme devotion gave,
Watching by his masters grave.
Then once more (so runs my tale)
To the restaurant owned by Traill
He repaired, by hunger driven,
And a tasty bun was given.
This became (to be explicit)
Quite a customary visit:
Daily, one the stroke of one,
Bobby went to claim his bun.
But no further would he roam —
Greyfriars Churchyard was his home!
With this simple fare content,
Back to guard the grave he went.

Years and seasons onward rolled:
Bobby would not be consoled.
Ever faithful he remained

And his ceaseless guard maintained.
Artists, hearing of his fame,
Oft to paint his portrait came.
Such rare charm did he possess
That a noble baroness,
Known for her philanthropy,
Truly was amazed to see
His outstanding loyal features
Rarely found in living creatures.
So at length when Bobby died
Tributes flowed from far and wide,
Showing how he was respected.
Then the baroness erected
A memorial effigy,
Cast in bronze, for all to see,
On a granite fountain based
And conspicuously placed,
Bobby to commemorate,
Near the Greyfriars Churchyard gate.

Bobby's memory lives today:
Still the Greyfriars people say
That, when nights are cold and drear,
Bobby's yelp they seem to hear!
'Neath the Edinburgh skies
Bobby near his master lies.
Still attentive passers-by
View his grave with moistened eye,
Pause and pay, with true emotion,
Tribute to a dog's devotion.

*Gilbert H. Brown*

# My Friend

Have you ever had a time when the tears roll down your face
And you need a special friend to be there to share the space.
A love so loyal and endless, the way we all should be,
A love with no conditions for all the world to see.

No matter where we travel, we're always side-by-side,
To keep me safe and happy and simply be my guide,
To share my inner secrets where very few have ever gone,
And never stand in judgment, that's why I wrote this song.

A friend like this is precious, one we should chance to meet,
To touch your very soul and help to make your life complete.
No complaints when times are troubled, just support and lots of love,
It's like an angel sent them, a gift from up above.

A greeting made of love every time is what you see,
And a smile to touch your heart and show the joy that's meant to be,
My special friend is with me every day and every year
And will always be remembered for a love so dear.

*Liana Preston*

# The Power of the Dog

There is sorrow enough in the natural way
From men and women to fill our day;
And when we are certain of sorrow in store,
Why do we always arrange for more?
Brothers and sisters, I bid you beware
Of giving your heart to a dog to tear.

Buy a pup and your money will buy
Love unflinching that cannot lie
Perfect passion and worship fed
By a kick in the ribs or a pat on the head.
Nevertheless it is hardly fair
To risk your heart for a dog to tear.

When the fourteen years which the Nature permits
Are closing in asthma, or tumour, or fits,
And the vet's unspoken prescription runs
To lethal chambers or loaded guns,
Then you will find – it's your own affair
But… you've given your heart to a dog to tear.

When the body that lived at your single will,
With it's whimper of welcome, is stilled (how still!)
When the spirit that answered your every mood
Is gone – wherever it goes – for good,
You will discover how much you care,
And will give your heart to a dog to tear!

We've sorrow enough in the natural way,
When it comes to buying Christian clay.
Our loves are not given, but only lent,
At compound interest of cent per cent,
Though it is not always the case, I believe,
That the longer we've kept'em, the more do we grieve,
For, when debts are payable, right or wrong,
A short-time loan is as bad as long –
So why in – Heaven (before we are there)
Should we give our hearts to a dog to tear?

*Joan Brownlee*

# The Presbytery Dog

Now all of the old sinners in mischief immersed,
From the ages of Gog and Magog,
At the top of the list, from the last to the first,
And by every good soul in the parish accursed,
Is that scamp of a Presbyt'ry Dog.

He's a hairy old scoundrel as ugly as sin,
He's a demon that travels incog,
With a classical name, and an ignorant grin,
And a tail, by the way, that is scraggy and thin,
And the rest of him merely a dog.

He is like a young waster of fortune possessed,
As he rambles the town at a jog;
For he treats the whole world as a sort of a jest,
While the comp'ny he keeps — well, it must be confessed
It's unfit for a Presbyt'ry Dog.

He is out on the street at the sound of a fight,
With the eyes of him standing agog,

And the scut of a tail — well, bedad, it's a fright:
Faith, you'd give him a kick that would set him alight,
But you can't with the Presbyt'ry Dog.

His rotundity now to absurdity runs,
Lie a black fellow gone to the grog:
For the knowing old shaver the presbyt'ry shuns
When it's time for a meal, and goes off to the nuns,
Who're deceived in the Presbyt'ry Dog.

When he follows the priest to the bush, there is war.
He inspects the whole place at a jog,
And he puts on great airs and fine antics galore,
While he chases the sheep till we're after his gore,
Though he may be the Presbyt'ry Dog.

'Twas last Sunday a dog in the church went ahead
With an ill-bred and loud monologue,
And the priest said some things that would shiver the dead,
And I'm with him in every last word that he said-
Ah, but wait — 'twas the Presbyt'ry Dog.

# To Jack The Toothless Terroriser!

Here at Bayview Vet Surgery
From dogs and cats and llamas
We meet our share of temperaments
From "cuddlies" to "piranhas"!

And though a grudge is never borne
And reputations falter
There is one lad, a J.R.T.
Whose manner never alters

He's tried and tried with all his might
To hang on to his dentures
To make sure he was well equipped
To meet with mis-adventure

And given hind sight on his side
He would have been more wary
Had he have heard the deal between
The vets and the tooth fairy

The fairy's house was fully built
The pool just made it heaven
To finish off the paving they
Would need more teeth – ELEVEN!

And so it came to be that Jack
Would donate to the cause
His loving nature as it is
He gave with open paws

So therein ends the myth that's told
Though sure that it will linger
That Austin & his staff take teeth
To merely keep their fingers!

# The Rubaiyat of a Scotch Terrier

Wake! For the sun wherin I love to snore
Has like an Eiderdown slid off me to the floor;
And I a drowsy step or two must creep
And flop into its gentle warmth once more.

Before my Beard from Breakfast scarce has dried,
Methinks a fretful Voice within me cried,
"When there are Puppy-Biscuits to prepare
Why tarries now that thoughtless Cook inside?"

And when the Clock strikes, yea, a bit before,
I yap impatient – "Open the door!
You can't fool *me*: I hear you scraping Plates;
And once that happens I can sleep no more."

And now the door is lockt; and I divine
They're having Tea! And softly first I whine,
Unheard by them whose festive Voices rise –
A moment more, you bet, they'll hear from *Mine!*

The Big Folk's Meal is done, the Pantry closed;
They'll get no more till Cook feels so disposed.
But still a Bone lies buried 'neath the Vines
For me, quite succulent though decomposed.

Come, fill the Cup; and in your hastening,
Your usual Conservatism fling.

I 'preciate your qualms (I'm Scotch myself)
But just this once, pray do the handsome Thing!

Ah, my Beloved, fill it to my Ears!
And do it while you can, for it appears
Our Milkman with the Housemaid down the road
Is now engrossed — and mayn't be back for Years.

Now lulled are gastronomical Desires:
A glutted Scot to Solitude retires;
Then Chafes to play, to *do* — but not alone:
It's Human Fellowship a dog requires.

Whether through something tactless I have done,
Whether to be Unfriendly I've begun,
I note, since I was bathed in Creolin,
My Paying Guests keep leaving one by one.

Of all three Words in Human Talk I know,
The three that animate me most I trow,
Have nought to do with Food, as you may think,
But form the welcome query "Want to go?"

The fondest Hope I set my heart upon
Is dashed when, though I have my Collar on,
The Door is shut without a word to me,
And You, with Hat and Walking-stick are gone.

Each Morn a lot of promises you say;
I know, but what of Yesterday
To take me for a Walk somewhere with You —
Then leave me sit and watch me go away.

Well, you can take them! What is that to me
(The Walks, I mean); but sorry you will be;'
You'll do it once to often one fine Day
And then come Home and find me dead – you'll see!

Some for the Plaudits of the Mob; and some
To anybody's flat'ring Call with come.
There's only One whose Patronage I crave,
And only One I take my orders from.

In making friends with me most People err;
at premature Caresses I demur
and quick resent familiarity;
Just let me do the wooing, as it were.

I'm racially conservative; my way
Is not on short Acquaintance to display
My Heart upon my Coat, but once I feel
You've passed my Muster I'm your friend for aye!

A row of Lamp-posts strung along the Street,
Sufficient Canine Friends of mine to greet,
A Shady Wall to sniff and contemplate –
Believe me, that were Paradise complete.

They say the tabby and The Tomcat take
Much Pleasure feigning sleep when they're awake,
Then scratch the Eyes of snooping dogs; - not mine:
I walk around them as I would a lake!

Think, in this batter'd Refuse Can to-day
what tempting Chicken-bones and Scrapings lay –
Fish-heads and other pleasing morsels fair –
Before the Dustman called – then went his way.

Myself when young did frequently frequent
My Mistress' Room and had great argument
With Shoes and Slippers mainly, but anon
Came out much faster than when I went.

For them I did the very best I could,
And tried with mine own Teeth to do them good;
And all the Harvest that I reap'd was Pain —
My Best intentions were aye misunderstood.

Oh, thou who once encouraged me, a Pup,
And thought it sporting when I tore things up,
Thou wilt not *now* chastise me before my Crime
And banish me to Bed before I sup?

Up from the Basement to my Master's Den
I plod; and patient watch him with a Pen
Forever scratching papers. There's a game
That's quite unfathomable to my Ken!

For there's the Door; the Sun is high; your free;
There is the whole wide World for us to see;
The Wind is calling us, yet you prefer
To sit and scratch — Oh, come along with me!

Strange, is it not? Of all the wondrous Things
Of Beauty, Joy and Love kind Heaven brings,
There's none so Wonderful as Mistress Mine —
And when I gaze at Her, my Heart just *sings.*

I sometimes think of what a cruel Joke
We Dogs in secret have on Human Folk
Who call themselves "superior," poor Dopes,
And yet all our Burdens bear the Yoke.

I once remember stopping in the Street,
And saw a Butcher fling a bit of Meat
Into the Sawdust rashly — and I cried,
"Pray, *Gently*, Brother, that is good to eat!"

However thrill'd you may be with Sabbath's Lark,
Pray keep you Dignity when in the Park.
Let shallow Dogs dash round in rings and yelp —
But if your Scotch, like me — you shall not bark.

A Ball practice makes for Eyes and Nose;
It's better through for Teeth and Paws and Toes;
Ask Him who throws it for me down the lawn:
He's bought them by the Dozen — and He Knows!

In Ecstasy I bite; and, having bit,
Chew on; nor all your strategy nor Wit
Can save its punctured Skin or spoil my Game,
For, bless you, that is half the Fun of it!

And that deflated Ball, so lately new,
Which gaily flashed and bounded as it flew,
Lift not your Hand to fling it more — for it
Is useless now — I don't know *why*, do you?

And this I know; it's never Sporting quite
To war on cats, or smaller Dogs to fight;
There's little Glory bruising Puss or Pom:
You'd better to an Airedale lose outright.

When Those-I-Love go out and say that they'll
Be back "in just a little while," I quail;
And though I sham indiff'rence when they come,
I cant help showing Gladness with my Tail.

'Tis but a Tail that takes but little rest
From wagging North and South or East and West
In Dog-talk: Friendship, Query, Hope, Assent,
According to the Mood to be expressed.

Why, if a purring Motor-car outside
Invites on the Air of Heav'n to ride,
Were't not a Shame — were't not a Shame for us
In this dull Habitation to abide?

A moments Halt, an unessential Waste,
Of precious Seconds — and we may be faced
With tragic Prospects, for the Taxi-man
May whisk away and leave us — Oh, make haste!

To lift one's Nose high in the Air,
And fel the grateful Wind trill through one's Hair:
Even on a Bus-top or in Taxi-cab,
Of all Adventures, none with this compare!

Yesterday this day's illness did prepare,
When I ate treach'rous Chicken-bones out there.
Now I in pain, with Held open wide,
Must drink! I know what or why — nor care!

Ah, with your Love my fading Life provide,
(To give you all of mine I've ever tried)
And lay me, when I've gone my longest Walk,
Deep down in my beloved Garden-side.

And when that Time comes, Master, if in vain
I seek a Paradise for Dogs, I fain
(If, as some say, there's no such Place for me)
Would dwell just in your Thoughts — and not complain.

And when along the Hallway you shall stroll,
Where I with patt'ring Feet soon often stole
With panting Tongue, and reach that Spot
Where I lapped long – turn down my empty Bowl!

*Sewell Collins*